CHANITA R. RAMSEY

As the Deer Pants After the Water

Letting Go of Toxic Love and Falling in Love with the One Who Never Left

INSPIRED
BY LOVE & GRACE
PUBLISHING

Contents

Introduction

I f you're holding this book, chances are your heart has been through some things—real things. You've loved deeply and lost painfully. You've held on to someone who didn't know how to hold you. Maybe you even questioned your worth in the process. And now, you're here… broken, tired, longing, and unsure of how to let go.

Let me begin by telling you something you may have never heard before: It was never God's intention for you to be wounded by love.

What hurt you was not love—it was a counterfeit. It was a distraction sent to keep you from discovering the fullness of what God has for you.

This book is more than words on a page—it's an invitation. A call to step away from the pain, the shame, the guilt, the resentment, and the loneliness. It's a challenge to confront the parts of you that have been surviving and invite healing into those places. It's a journey we'll take together—one that leads you back to the heart of the One who made you, knows you, and still desires you.

God has not forgotten you. He's not angry with you. He's not disappointed in your past or surprised by your struggles. He's waiting. Waiting to heal you, love you, restore you, and reveal the truth about who you are and whose you are.

This book was created to be a safe space—where you can cry, question, release, reflect, and heal. A space where you can learn to recognize the lies of the enemy, expose the traps of toxic love, and stop settling for less than what God intended for you. You were never meant to be stuck in cycles of pain. You were meant to walk in freedom.

So, I invite you to come boldly and honestly. Bring your wounds. Bring your fears. Bring your whole heart.

Let's go on this journey together—one step at a time—as we uncover the beauty of falling in love with God, the only One who will never mishandle your heart.

You are not too far gone. You are not too broken. You are not forgotten. You are His. And He's calling you back to the place where your soul can breathe again.

Let the healing begin.

Devotional Reflection: Letting Go to Be Found

Before we begin this journey, pause and take a deep breath. Let this be your first sacred moment of surrender.

Think about what you've been carrying—the heartbreak, the questions, the shame, the longing, the guilt. Maybe you've tried to move on, but something still pulls you back. Maybe you've forgiven them but haven't yet forgiven yourself. Or maybe you've stopped hoping altogether.

God sees every layer of that pain—and He's not asking you to pretend it didn't happen. He's asking you to let Him into it.

Letting go doesn't mean you're weak. It means you're brave enough to trust that healing is possible.

This is not about rushing your process—it's about beginning it. And you don't have to walk it alone.

As the deer pants after the water, so your soul pants after something more. That "more" is Him. And He's here now, welcoming you home.

Opening Prayer:

Father,

I come to You with everything that I am and everything that I've been through.

You know the hurt I carry... the wounds from loving someone who couldn't love me back the way I needed.

You know the ways I've tried to fill the emptiness with things that never satisfied.

But today, I choose something different.

I choose You.

Help me to let go of what has broken me.

Unclench my fists from the pain, the shame, the anger, and the guilt.

Uncover the lies I've believed about myself and show me the truth of who I am in You.

Father, I want to fall in love with You again—maybe for the first time in a real, deep way.

I want to be whole. I want to be free.

So, lead me step by step, word by word, back to Your heart.

Thank You for still desiring me.

Thank You for Your everlasting love.

Thank You for never giving up on me.

In Jesus' name,

Amen.

Chapter One: A Love That Hurts

Why It's So Hard to Let Go

When What You Thought Was Love Leaves You Broken

You didn't go looking for pain.

You were just looking for love.

The kind of love that makes you feel seen, chosen, and pursued.

The kind you dreamed about, prayed for, and hoped would finally feel safe.

But somewhere along the way, what looked like love became something else—

something twisted, confusing, and quietly destructive.

By the time you realized it, your heart was already entangled.

Toxic love doesn't always announce itself with cruelty.

Sometimes it whispers just enough hope to keep you holding on.

It gives you moments of joy wrapped in cycles of pain.

It pulls you close—only to push you away again.

It makes you question your worth, your sanity, even your identity.

And the longer you stay, the harder it becomes to remember who you were before it began.

Maybe you ignored the red flags because your heart was hungry to be chosen.

Maybe you thought love meant sacrificing everything—your voice, your boundaries, your needs.

Maybe deep down, you didn't believe you deserved anything better.

But God saw it all.

And He wasn't standing in judgment—

He was standing in love, ready to rescue you from what was never meant to keep you bound.

You were not created for confusion.

You were not created for emotional chaos.

You were created for love—

but not the kind that wounds you. The kind that restores you.

The Trap of Toxic Love

Toxic love is often rooted in trauma.

It mirrors back the parts of us that haven't yet healed.

That's why it can feel familiar—even when it hurts.

We stay because we're hoping for a different ending.

We keep trying because we believe love should be patient, forgiving, enduring.

But trauma-driven love doesn't heal—it cycles.

It keeps us attached to relationships that replay childhood wounds, abandonment, rejection, and neglect.

And the enemy knows exactly how to exploit that.

He knows how to package bondage to look like passion.

He knows how to dress dysfunction up as destiny.

He knows how to hide chains behind charm.

But what he didn't count on...

was that God would interrupt your story and wake you up.

This is your awakening moment.

You don't have to stay in what broke you.

You don't have to carry shame for what you didn't know.

You don't have to keep pouring love into someone who only takes and leaves you empty.

God wants your heart whole.

And healing begins with truth—
this wasn't love, and it never was.

Scenarios: Recognizing Toxic Love

You stayed because he said he needed you—but never once asked what you needed.

You became the rescuer, the therapist, the fixer. You were never allowed to simply be the woman who wanted to be loved back.

You tried to be "low maintenance" so he wouldn't leave.

You silenced your voice, minimized your needs, and settled for breadcrumbs of affection—while starving emotionally.

You mistook chaos for passion, believing love was supposed to hurt a little.

You became addicted to the highs and lows because peace felt unfamiliar. Now you realize—it wasn't love. It was trauma.

You waited for years, thinking he would change.

Thinking your love would finally be enough to fix him.

Instead, you lost yourself—while he stayed the same.

Divine Reassurance

You are not weak for staying.
You are not foolish for believing.
You are not broken beyond repair.
God sees the layers of your heart.
He knows what you endured.
And He is not disappointed in you.
You are not alone in this awakening.
God is not watching from a distance—
He is sitting with you in the truth, the grief, and the realization.
You are not forgotten.
You are being rebuilt.
Let the exposure become freedom.

Let the truth become healing.

Let this be the moment you choose wholeness.

A Word from the Father's Heart

"My daughter, I saw you when you cried yourself to sleep.

I heard the prayers you whispered in the dark.

You thought I was silent—but I was watching, grieving with you, and waiting.

Waiting for the moment you would realize you are worth more than this.

I never designed love to make you feel small.

I made you to be loved fully—without fear, without confusion, without pain.

Come back to Me.

Let Me show you what love really looks like."

Reflection

Toxic love doesn't trap you overnight—it entangles you slowly.

It feeds on hope, fear, and unhealed wounds.

Recognizing it is not condemnation—it's clarity.

And clarity is the doorway to freedom.

This chapter isn't meant to shame you.

It's meant to awaken you.

Journal Prompt

- What parts of this chapter resonated most deeply with your own experience?
- What red flags did you ignore—and why?
- What lies about love or your worth kept you staying longer than you should have?
- Write a letter to yourself acknowledging what you didn't know then—and

honoring the strength it took to see the truth now.

Prayer

Father,

Help me see clearly.

I've been tangled in a love that wasn't love at all.

I confess that I stayed in places that hurt me because I didn't believe I deserved better.

But today, I choose truth.

I choose healing.

I choose to believe that You have more for me.

Heal the wounds I've been hiding.

Break every soul tie that keeps me bound.

And help me walk away—not with bitterness, but with freedom.

Teach me how to love myself the way You love me.

In Jesus' name, Amen.

Closing Quote

"Awareness is not rejection—it's rescue. When God opens your eyes, it's because freedom is within reach."

Chapter Two: When Love Leaves You Empty

The soul-toll of staying too long in broken places

You thought it was love.

You gave your all.

You poured from a full cup until you had nothing left—and still, it wasn't enough.

Now you're left sitting in the ruins of what you thought was forever, trying to make sense of the silence that follows the goodbye. But the truth is, the silence didn't start when they left. It started long before that—when you were lying beside someone who made you feel completely alone.

The worst kind of loneliness isn't always being by yourself.

It's being connected to someone who never truly sees you.

Scenarios: When Love Leaves You Empty

- You stayed because he said he needed you—but never once asked what you needed.
- You became the rescuer, the therapist, the mother, the fixer. You were never just allowed to be the woman who wanted to be loved back.
- You tried to be "low maintenance"—easy to love—so he wouldn't leave.

- You silenced your voice, minimized your needs, and settled for bread-crumbs of affection. In return, you got emotional starvation.
- You mistook chaos for passion, thinking love was supposed to hurt a little.
- You were addicted to the highs and lows because you never experienced peace that felt like home. Now you realize—it was trauma, not love.
- You waited for years, thinking he'd change, thinking your love would be enough to fix him.
- Instead, you lost yourself while he stayed the same.

The Aftermath of Letting Go

Now that it's over, the quiet is deafening. You're no longer crying over the relationship—but there's a hollow space where hope used to live. This is the grief that no one talks about: the grief of walking away from someone who wasn't good for you, but still left a hole in your soul.

Loneliness is real. And it's not always a sign that you did something wrong—it's a sign that you need healing. That you're detoxing from something you were never supposed to be attached to.

But here's the truth: God can do His best work in the empty places.

When everything else is stripped away—when no one's calling, when the bed feels too big, when your phone stays silent—it's in that space that God begins to whisper your true name.

He doesn't just want to comfort your loneliness. He wants to transform it.

Divine Reassurance

You are not alone in your letting go.

God is not only watching from a distance—He is sitting with you in the quiet, the tears, the ache.

You are not forgotten. You are being rebuilt.

Let the loneliness become sacred ground where your soul learns to crave Him more than the counterfeit.

A Word from the Father's Heart

"My daughter, I know the ache you carry. I see the empty spaces no one else sees.

You thought you lost everything, but what you lost was making room for Me.

Let Me fill the hollow places. Let Me restore what was taken.

You were never meant to feel invisible in love. You were created to be fully seen, fully known, and fully cherished—by Me."

Prayer:

Father,

I admit—I feel the weight of this emptiness.

I miss what I had, even though it hurt me.

I feel lonely, and I don't always know what to do with that feeling.

But I choose to believe that You are with me, even in this.

Help me not to run back out of fear or desperation.

Teach me how to sit in the stillness and find You here.

Fill every hollow space with Your love.

I trust You to make me whole again.

In Jesus' name,

Amen.

Reflection:

Loneliness after letting go is not a punishment—it's part of the healing process. It reveals how much of ourselves we poured into someone who was never meant to be our source. It's okay to feel the emptiness. It's okay to miss what you walked away from. But it's also okay to believe that the space left behind is an invitation—an opening for God to pour something deeper and more lasting into your heart. This is not the end of your story. This is where your real healing begins.

Journal Prompt:

- What are the emotions you're experiencing now that the relationship has ended?
- What lies about yourself or your worth are trying to surface in your loneliness?
- How can you begin to shift your view of this lonely season into a sacred time of restoration?
- Write a letter to God, pouring out every raw feeling—anger, sadness, confusion, fear. Then ask Him to show you where He is in the midst of it.

Prayer:

Lord,

The silence is loud, and the nights feel long.

There are moments I want to run back to what was familiar—even if it wasn't good for me.

But I know You are calling me higher.

Help me to sit with the ache without numbing it.

Teach me how to trust You in the waiting.

Help me believe that this space of emptiness is not a void, but a vessel You're about to fill.

Wrap me in Your presence when I feel alone.

Speak to the wounded parts of me that still long to be loved.

I surrender this loneliness to You.

Amen.

Closing Quote:

"Sometimes God has to empty your hands so He can fill them with something sacred. Don't rush back to what broke you—let Him fill you with a love that heals."

Chapter Three: Craving Love, Needing Healing

Why Your Longing for Love Doesn't Make You Weak—it Makes You Human

Y ou were made to love.

You were created for connection, closeness, and intimacy.

You were designed with a heart that desires to give and receive love.

There is nothing wrong with that.

But when your longing for love goes unmet—or is repeatedly mishandled—it creates a deep ache in your soul. And if that ache goes unhealed, it can quietly drive your decisions.

An unhealed heart doesn't search for wholeness.

It searches for relief.

It reaches for anything that promises comfort—even if that comfort costs you peace later.

That's how people end up settling for what they once said they'd never tolerate.

This is why healing matters.

Because pain that isn't healed will eventually choose for you.

When Longing Turns into Vulnerability

Some days, you're strong.

You're full of faith, standing on God's promises, reminding yourself that He's working things out.

And other days… you're exhausted.

Tired of being patient.

Tired of being alone.

Tired of feeling like everyone else has what you're still praying for.

And that doesn't make you weak.

God is not disappointed by your humanity—He welcomes it.

But what He doesn't want is for your pain to become permanent.

Loneliness has a way of making old doors look appealing again.

It tempts you to return to what's familiar—even when familiar was harmful.

This is where the enemy works hardest.

He whispers lies like:

"You'll always be alone."

"This is as good as it gets."

"You're too damaged to wait for more."

"At least he gave you some attention."

And if you're not rooted in healing, those lies start sounding like truth.

Choosing Contentment in the Process

Healing doesn't always feel good—but it produces something good.

It teaches you how to:

- Be stable without a relationship
- Be fulfilled without constant attention
- Be secure without external validation
- And that contentment becomes your protection.

Because when you're content:

- You stop chasing what's toxic.
- You stop entertaining distractions.
- You stop falling for the same trap wrapped in a different body.
- You begin to crave peace more than passion.

You learn how to wait on God instead of running ahead of Him.

Your desire for love is not wrong.

It simply needs to be **re-centered in Him**.

Divine Perspective

Longing doesn't mean you're lacking faith.

It means you're human.

But God never intended for your desire to lead you into bondage.

He intended it to draw you closer to Him.

When your heart is anchored in God:

- You stop using people to fill God-sized voids.
- You stop settling for partial love.
- You stop confusing attention with affection.

Healing doesn't remove desire.

It places desire in its proper order.

A Word from the Father's Heart

"My daughter, I placed the desire for love inside of you.

But I never intended for that desire to lead you into bondage.

Let Me show you how to love without losing yourself.

Let Me teach you what it means to be cherished without compromise.

You don't have to numb your longing—I want to fulfill it.

But I will not compete with your idols.

Lay your heart in My hands,

and watch Me heal what you thought was unfixable."

Reflection

The desire to be loved is deeply human—God placed it in you.

But only He can fulfill it in a way that leaves you whole instead of hollow.

When you learn to be content in His love first, relationships stop being a source of validation and start becoming a place of overflow.

From that place of peace, you'll recognize the counterfeit for what it is—and wait for what's real.

Journal Prompt

- In what areas have you been trying to fill a God-sized void with people, attention, or relationships?
- What lies has the enemy been whispering to you in your vulnerable moments?
- What would contentment look like for you in this season—even while you're still healing?
- Write a personal declaration reclaiming your peace, your value, and your commitment to wait on God's best.

Prayer

God,

I confess that I've tried to soothe my pain in the wrong places.

I've craved love so deeply that I almost forgot where real love comes from.

Today, I bring You every unmet need, every longing, every ache.

Teach me how to be still in Your presence.

Help me not to rush this process or settle out of fear.

Let contentment rise in my spirit—even when I don't understand everything.

Fill me so deeply that I no longer feel desperate for what cannot satisfy.

Make me whole, Lord.
Amen.

Closing Quote

"Your craving for love doesn't make you weak—it makes you human. But trusting God with that craving is what makes you whole."

Healing Exercise: Sitting in the Pain, Pressing Through the Process

P urpose:
   To help you confront, process, and release emotional pain from toxic love and past trauma, and to anchor your strength in God's presence—even in the silence and loneliness.

Step 1: Create a Safe Space

- Find a quiet, undistracted space—somewhere you feel physically and emotionally safe.
- Bring a journal, a pen, and your Bible.
- Light a candle or play soft worship music if that helps you feel connected to God.

Say aloud:
   "This is my healing space. God is here with me. I am safe."

Step 2: Name the Pain

In your journal, answer honestly:

- What hurt me the most in that toxic relationship or traumatic experience?
- What do I still carry in my heart from that season?

• What lies did I begin to believe about myself because of that pain?

Be raw. Be honest. God can handle it.

Then write this declaration at the bottom of the page:

"This pain is real, but it will not define me."

Step 3: Sit in the Pain

Close your eyes. Take deep, slow breaths. Feel the heaviness—but don't run from it.

Say to yourself (or aloud):

• "It's okay to feel this."
• "God is with me in this moment."
• "I don't have to fix it all today—I just have to show up."

Let yourself cry if you need to. Weep. Whisper. Be still. This is your moment of sacred release.

Step 4: Press Through in Prayer

Now talk to God. Say what you feel—every word, even the ugly ones.

Then, when you've poured it out, speak this prayer:

"Lord, I am not okay—and I'm finally being honest about it.

I've carried so much pain, so much shame, and so much loneliness.

I wanted to run from it, bury it, or fill it with distractions.

But today, I'm sitting in it—so You can heal it.

Help me not just to survive, but to press through.

I trust You to walk with me through the valley.

Even in the pain, You are still good.

I give You every piece of me. Every broken place. Every wound.

Now show me how to breathe again."

Step 5: Write a Release Letter

On a fresh page, write a letter starting with:

"God, I'm letting go of…"

Then pour out every name, situation, memory, emotion, and pain you're choosing to release today.

End your letter with:

"I choose healing. I choose freedom. I choose You."

Tear the page out. Fold it. Pray over it. And if you're ready—burn it, bury it, or throw it away. Do something physical to represent the spiritual release.

Closing Scripture Meditation:

Read slowly and reflect on Isaiah 43:2-3 (NLT):

"When you go through deep waters, I will be with you.

When you go through rivers of difficulty, you will not drown.

When you walk through the fire of oppression, you will not be burned up; the flames will not consume you.

For I am the Lord, your God, the Holy One of Israel, your Savior."

Affirmation to Speak Over Yourself:

"I am healing. I am not who I used to be. I will not go back.

Even in the pain, I am pressing through, and I am not alone."

Chapter Four: Alone but Not Abandoned

Walking Through the Wilderness of Loneliness with God by Your Side

Loneliness has a way of making you feel like you're being punished for choosing healing.

You finally walked away.

You finally stopped answering the late-night calls.

You finally admitted the truth: what you were clinging to was breaking you.

And yet... now it feels quiet.

Quiet mornings.

Quiet evenings.

Quiet phone.

Quiet bed.

Quiet mind—except for the thoughts that get loud when nobody's there to distract you.

This is the part nobody prepares you for: the wilderness after letting go.

Not the wilderness where you're fighting the relationship.

But the wilderness where you're fighting *yourself*—your cravings, your memories, your emotions, and the fear that you'll always be alone.

But hear this clearly:

Being alone is not the same as being abandoned.

You may be walking through a lonely season, but you are not unloved, unseen, or forgotten. God is with you—especially here.

When the Wilderness Feels Like Rejection

The wilderness can feel like God stepped back. Like He got quiet. Like He left you to figure it out.

But the truth is, God often does His deepest work in the in-between.

The wilderness is where:

- Your identity gets rooted in Him—not in validation.
- Your soul detoxes from emotional addiction.
- Your discernment gets sharpened.
- Your boundaries get strengthened.
- Your healing gets protected.

This season may feel empty, but it's not pointless.

The wilderness is not punishment. It's preparation.

Avoiding the Pitfalls of the Wilderness

This season of loneliness can be dangerous—not because of the silence, but because of what the silence tempts you to do.

Loneliness will tempt you to go back:

- Back to the relationship you prayed your way out of.
- Back to the situations God delivered you from.
- Back to the thing that was broken—but familiar.

But let this truth anchor you:

Familiar does not equal safe.

Comfortable does not equal healthy.

The enemy doesn't always attack with chaos. Sometimes he attacks with nostalgia.

He'll remind you of the good times—but never the wounds.

He'll replay the memories—but erase the manipulation.

He'll whisper, *"At least you weren't alone."*

But going back will cost you more this time—because now you know better.

You've tasted healing.

You've started waking up.

You've come too far to trade your freedom for temporary comfort.

Loneliness is a feeling, not a destination.

Don't let a temporary emotion make a permanent decision.

Stay in the Process

You cannot skip this part.

The wilderness is where God teaches you how to stand without leaning on people who were never meant to hold you up. It's where He shows you that peace is possible—even without a relationship.

If you skip the wilderness, you'll step into your next season:

- still bleeding,
- still craving,
- still easily attached,
- still vulnerable to counterfeits.

But if you stay with God in the process, you'll come out different:

- wiser,
- stronger,
- stable,
- and whole enough to recognize real love when it comes.

Wisdom Keys to Survive the Wilderness Without Falling Back

1. **Stay connected to God—even when it feels dry.**
2. Dry seasons don't mean God is gone. They mean you're being strengthened.
3. **Write down what God has already delivered you from.**
4. When you're tempted, don't romanticize your bondage—remember the truth.
5. **Surround yourself with truth-tellers.**
6. Have at least one person who can remind you who you are when your emotions try to rewrite history.
7. **Don't medicate your loneliness with people.**
8. Numbing delays healing. God wants to *transform* the lonely places—not just help you escape them.
9. **Let the wilderness become holy ground.**
10. This is where your soul learns to crave Him more than the counterfeit.

A Word from the Father's Heart

"My daughter, you are not forgotten.
I'm walking with you through every dry place.
When you feel the most alone, I'm holding you the closest.
Don't fear the silence—it's where I speak the loudest.
You may not feel strong, but I see the warrior I created in you.
Keep going. I'm with you in the wilderness, and I will not leave you there."

Reflection

Being alone and being abandoned are two different things. You may be in a lonely season, but you are not unloved, unseen, or uncared for.

God is with you—even when your emotions say otherwise.

And the wilderness may feel like a wasteland, but in God's hands, it becomes **sacred ground**.

Journal Prompt

- What does your "wilderness" feel like right now? (Be specific.)
- Where are you most tempted to go backward—and why?
- What do you believe God is trying to heal or strengthen in you in this season?
- Write a letter to God expressing your fears. Then write a letter back from God's perspective—speaking courage and truth over you.

Prayer

God,
　This place feels lonely and unfamiliar.
　Sometimes I wonder if You hear me, or if You're really near.
　But even in my doubt, I choose to believe Your promise:
　You will never leave me nor forsake me.
　Give me strength for the middle place.
　Help me keep walking through this wilderness with confidence,
　knowing You are right beside me—even when I can't feel You.
　Thank You for seeing something in me I don't yet see in myself.
　I trust You to lead me through.
　In Jesus' name, Amen.

Closing Quote

"You may feel alone, but you've never been abandoned. God doesn't just deliver you—He walks with you every step of the way."

Closing Scripture Meditation

Read slowly and reflect on **Isaiah 43:2–3 (NLT):**
　"When you go through deep waters, I will be with you… For I am the Lord, your God…"

Affirmation to Speak Over Yourself

"I am healing. I am not who I used to be. I will not go back.
   Even in the pain, I am pressing through—and I am not alone."

Chapter Five: Why You Shouldn't Settle

The danger of rebound relationships and the beauty of waiting on God

L et's be honest: waiting on God isn't easy.

It gets lonely.

It gets quiet.

It gets frustrating.

Sometimes, it feels like everyone else has someone, and you're left sitting in the silence with your wounds and unanswered prayers. In those moments, your mind may whisper, "Maybe I'm being too picky," or "Maybe a little love is better than no love at all."

But here's the truth: settling for what looks like love will only delay the love God actually designed for you.

Rebound Love Is a Risky Escape

After leaving a toxic relationship, your soul is bruised, and your heart craves comfort. That's when rebound relationships look the most appealing—someone to distract you, affirm you, or fill the empty space. But don't confuse relief with restoration.

Rebounds aren't about healing—they're about escaping.

They may give you temporary attention, but not true connection.

They may help you forget, but they won't help you heal.

What feels good for the moment can cause long-term damage to a heart that's still in recovery.

What You Desire Will Either Lead You to God—or Away from Him

Any desire that isn't rooted in Christ will eventually pull you away from Him. That's why the enemy works overtime to distort your hunger for love. He'll send counterfeits when you're most vulnerable—distracting you from the very One who loved you first, and loves you best.

The Word says in 1 John 4:19, "We love because He first loved us."

Your love life must be grounded in His love, not driven by your loneliness.

When your heart is anchored in God, you begin to crave wholeness, not just affection.

Don't Rush What God Is Still Preparing

Waiting doesn't mean God forgot you. It means He's preparing you—and the one He has for you—for a love that will glorify Him.

Settling might give you something now.

But waiting will give you what lasts.

And anything worth having is worth the wait.

From the Father's Heart

"My daughter, I see your tears. I see your longing. I know it feels like you've waited long enough. But I'm not withholding love from you—I'm protecting you.

What I give you will not come with confusion, pain, or compromise.

Don't settle for what's easy.

Wait for what's holy.

I'm preparing a love story that reflects My heart for you.

Trust Me with the pen."

Reflection:

- Have you ever felt tempted to settle for less than God's best just to avoid being alone?
- What lies have you believed about God's timing or your worth that need to be surrendered?

Journal Prompt:

- Write about a time when settling brought more pain than peace. What did you learn from that experience?
- Now write a letter to your future self, reminding her to wait on God, even when it's hard.

Prayer:

Father,
  I've been tempted to settle. I've been tired of waiting.
  But I don't want to trade my healing for a moment of comfort.
  Remind me of who I am in You, and what I'm truly worth.
  Help me to stay grounded in Your love,
  and trust that Your timing is perfect—even when it doesn't feel that way.
  Teach me to be content in Your presence.
  And when love comes, let it be a reflection of Your heart.
  Amen.

Closing Quote:

"You don't need a placeholder for the love God is preparing. You just need the patience to wait."

Chapter Six: When Flesh Fights Faith

Wrestling with desire while trying to please God

There comes a moment—sometimes more than once—when you feel the full weight of your humanity. When the desire to feel wanted, to be held, to be seen, becomes louder than the promise you made to yourself to heal. When your body remembers what it once had, even if your spirit knows it was never holy.

This is the war between flesh and faith.

It's in the text thread you want to send.

The late-night thoughts.

The loneliness that makes you question if walking away was even worth it.

It's a real war. And you're not weak because you feel it. You're human. But you are not without help.

The Spirit Is Willing… But the Flesh Is Loud

In Matthew 26:41, Jesus told His disciples, "The spirit is willing, but the flesh is weak." He wasn't condemning them—He was understanding them.

The pull of the past isn't always about a person—it's about the emotional, physical, and soul-level cravings that person awakened in you. But when those cravings show up, they don't come alone. They bring shame, guilt, and spiritual warfare with them.

This is the tug-of-war between your desire and your destiny.

When the Whisper Is Stronger Than the Craving

Let's talk about those moments where the Holy Spirit stepped in:

Tamika, who used to cry herself to sleep after her ex would cheat and gaslight her, found herself one night scrolling through his social media. The urge to reach out nearly overtook her. But in the silence of her room, she heard it: "You promised you'd never go back." And right then, her tears shifted—from craving to conviction. She blocked the number and picked up her Bible instead.

Sharon, who battled feelings of unworthiness, got a message from the very man God delivered her from. He was apologetic, said all the right things. She considered meeting him. But as she put on her shoes, she heard in her spirit: "Would you trade your healing for one more broken night?" She sat down, cried for an hour—and stayed home.

You've had moments like that too.

Moments where your spirit stepped in and saved you from what your flesh was prepared to walk into.

That's the Holy Spirit.

That's God's love.

That's your growth.

The Power on the Inside of You

Don't believe the lie that you're too weak to overcome. Romans 8:11 says, "The same Spirit that raised Christ from the dead dwells in you." That's not a poetic idea—it's a real power that lives in your spirit.

You don't fight this battle alone.

Every time you say no to what your flesh wants and yes to what your faith believes, heaven stands with you.

There may be tears.

There may be shaking hands.

But there is also VICTORY—even if it comes in small steps.

From the Father's Heart

"My daughter, I see the war inside you. I hear your cries when no one else does. I know the weight of your desire. But I promise, if you trust Me, I will fill every empty place you thought only a person could fill. I will meet you in your weakness and remind you that My strength is made perfect there. You are not alone in this fight. I am the One who makes you strong."

Reflection:

- What situations or feelings most often trigger the battle between your flesh and your faith?
- Can you recall a time when the Holy Spirit helped you walk away from something that would've delayed your healing?

Journal Prompt:

- Write about a time when you wanted to give in—but you didn't. What helped you stay strong?
- Now, write a declaration that begins: "Even when I'm weak, the Spirit within me is…"

Prayer:

Holy Spirit,
  You know the war within me.
  You know the places where my flesh screams and my faith trembles.
  But I choose You.
  I choose healing.
  I choose wholeness over temporary comfort.
  Strengthen me in my weakness.
  Speak louder than my cravings.
  Let my life reflect a love that chooses You—over and over again.

Amen.

Closing Quote:

"Temptation may knock, but your spirit doesn't have to answer. There's power in your no."

Chapter Seven: He Still Wants You

The unimaginable depth of God's pursuit—even when you turn away

You might not believe this right now, but it's true:

God still wants you.

Not the cleaned-up, perfect, got-it-all-together version of you.

You.

The broken you.

The hurting you.

The ashamed you.

The confused, distant, backslidden, angry, disappointed, and weary you.

He still wants you. And He hasn't changed His mind.

You Are Always On His Mind

Psalm 8:4 says, "What is man that You are mindful of him?"

That word mindful means God's thoughts are full of you.

Let that sink in.

He doesn't visit your life occasionally. His mind stays full of you.

He watches your tears fall.

He sees the hidden fears you can't tell anyone.

He hears the cries of your soul that never leave your lips.

And He loves you still.

Love That Doesn't Leave

We've been conditioned by human relationships—conditional love, inconsistent affection, love that walks away when we mess up. But God's love is on a different level.

He is not afraid of your mess.

In fact, He steps into it—again and again.

Even when you walk away from Him, He walks toward you.

Psalm 139:8 says, "If I make my bed in hell, behold, You are there."

That's not poetic imagery—that's covenant love.

He's not just concerned about your church attendance or your spiritual gifts.

He's concerned about the whole you—your emotions, your body, your mind, your relationships, your healing. He's the God who counts your tears and holds every piece of your heart in His hands.

You Can't Scare God Away

Maybe you've turned your back on God.

Maybe you've gone back to something He freed you from.

Maybe you're reading this feeling unworthy of another chance.

But here's the truth:

You couldn't make God stop loving you if you tried.

Jeremiah 31:3 says, "I have loved you with an everlasting love."

Everlasting means without beginning or end.

That means His love never started, and it will never stop.

When Love Pursues You

Let's be real: some days you don't feel lovable.

Your past haunts you.

Your choices shame you.

But God doesn't love you based on your behavior—He loves you because of who He is.

He is love.

It reminds us of the story of the prodigal son (Luke 15).

He walked away. Wasted everything. And when he decided to come back home, the father was already watching for him.

When the father saw him "a long way off," he ran to him. He didn't wait for an apology. He didn't shame him.

He welcomed him back with open arms.

That's what God does every time we turn back to Him.

From the Father's Heart

"My daughter, I saw the moment your heart broke. I heard the silent cries you thought no one noticed. I never stopped loving you. Not for one second. I'm still here—arms wide open, heart full of grace. I want you. I want all of you. Not just your worship. Not just your obedience. I want your laughter. Your tears. Your questions. Your fears. I want to walk with you again. Come home. I've never stopped waiting."

Reflection:

- Have you ever felt like you had to "clean yourself up" before returning to God?
- What parts of your life have you believed were too messy for God to want?

Journal Prompt:

- Write a letter from God to yourself, based on what you now know about His love. Let it flow freely—no filters, no shame. Let it be a love letter to your weary heart.

Prayer:

Father,

Thank You for loving me even when I didn't love myself.

Thank You for wanting me even when I walked away.

Your love is bigger than my failure.

It's stronger than my shame.

Help me rest in the truth that I am still Yours.

No matter what I've done.

I come home to You.

Amen.

Closing Quote:

"God's love doesn't flinch at your flaws—it pursues you through them.

Chapter Eight: Everlasting Love

Learning to receive a love that doesn't change with your behavior

What if everything you believed about love had conditions tied to it?

What if your entire life, love meant earning it, performing for it, begging to keep it, or apologizing for not being enough for it?

When you've only known love that shifts with moods, wounds, or worthiness, it's hard to trust a love that promises to stay—especially when you mess up.

But God's love isn't like theirs.

God's love doesn't shift.

It doesn't shut down.

It doesn't walk away when you're not at your best.

This Love Is Different

The world taught you that love could be lost—

that one mistake could make someone stop caring…

that one wrong move could turn passion into punishment.

But God's love is not moved by mood swings.

It is not based on how spiritual you feel, how perfect you act, or how much you "deserve" it.

The Lord said, "I have loved you with an everlasting love. I have drawn you with unfailing kindness." (Jeremiah 31:3)

That means before the heartbreak, before the toxic relationship, before the abandonment—He loved you.

And now, in your healing, your wrestling, your wondering, He still does.

You Don't Have to Earn This

Some of us treat God like He's keeping score.

We think if we cry enough, clean up enough, or prove ourselves enough, He'll "really" love us. But that's not how this relationship works.

You're not auditioning for the Father's affection.

You're already chosen.

Already desired.

Already called beloved.

The blood of Jesus settled it—once and for all.

You're not loved because of what you do.

You're loved because of who He is.

When You Feel Unlovable

Some days, you don't even like yourself.

You know your flaws, your temper, your doubts.

You know the thoughts you think but don't speak, the pain you hide, the sins you keep silent.

And yet—He still loves you.

God doesn't run from the mess.

He walks into it.

He sits in it with you.

And He patiently reminds you that nothing you've done has changed His mind about you.

Let It Sink In

His love isn't just everlasting. It's unchanging.

When you're faithful—He loves you.

When you fall—He loves you.

When you worship—He loves you.

When you doubt—He loves you.

There's nothing you can do to increase His love, and nothing you can do to make it disappear. He set His heart on you before you ever said yes to Him.

You are His. And He is yours. Forever.

From the Father's Heart

"You don't have to chase Me down or convince Me to stay.

My love for you is not on a timer.

It does not rise and fall with your performance.

Even on your worst days, I call you Mine.

Let My love wrap around your wounds and silence every voice that told you you were unworthy of it.

I'm not going anywhere. I never was."

Reflection:

- What conditional patterns of love have you carried into your view of God?
- Do you believe you're lovable even when you're not "doing everything right"?
- What part of God's love feels hardest to receive?

Journal Prompt:

- Write about the first time you remember feeling like love was based on performance. Then contrast it with what God says about His everlasting love in Jeremiah 31:3.
- What truth is He asking you to embrace today?

Prayer:

Lord,

I've been afraid to trust in love that doesn't change.

I've been taught that love walks away, that it gets tired, that it leaves when I don't measure up.

But You're different.

Teach me how to receive Your love, even when I don't feel worthy of it.

Heal every place in me that was trained to expect rejection.

Let Your everlasting love be the foundation of my healing.

Amen.

Closing Quote:

"You are not too inconsistent to be loved by a consistent God."

Healing Exercise: "Let Love Find You Here"

Allowing yourself to receive God's love exactly where you are

Purpose:

This exercise is about learning to sit in the truth that you are wanted, pursued, and cherished by God—not for what you've done, but for who you are. It will help dismantle the lie that you must earn His love, and invite His presence into your present reality.

Step 1: Create Sacred Space

Find a quiet, comfortable space where you can be alone with your thoughts. Light a candle, turn on soft worship music, or sit in stillness—whatever helps you feel safe and centered.

Step 2: Write a Confession Without Judgment

On paper, or in your journal, write down:

- The things you've felt made you "unlovable" or "too broken" for God.
- The moments you walked away from Him.
- The places you feel most ashamed, most rejected, or most hidden.

Don't hold back. Be raw. Be honest. This is not a space for shame—this is a sacred offering.

Then underneath it all, write this phrase:

"He still wants me."

Step 3: Imagine His Embrace

Close your eyes and envision Jesus standing in front of you—not angry, not disappointed, but full of compassion.

Hear Him say to you:

"I still want you. I always have. I never stopped loving you, and I never will."

Let those words wash over you.

Step 4: Let Him Hold You There

Sit with Him in that space.

Cry if you need to.

Breathe deeply.

Don't rush the moment.

Let His love do what only it can do—heal what no one else sees.

Step 5: Declare This Over Yourself

Say this out loud or write it in your journal:

"I am not too broken. I am not too far gone. God still wants me. I receive His love today—not because I earned it, but because it's who He is."

Optional Scripture Meditation:

Read and reflect on Luke 15:20, Psalm 139:7–10, Romans 8:38–39.

Chapter Nine: You Were Always on His Mind

Discovering how much God truly treasures and thinks of you

H ave you ever wondered if anyone truly sees you?

Not just the version of you who smiles and keeps it together—but the parts of you that feel forgotten, misunderstood, and overlooked?

You've sat in rooms full of people and felt invisible.

You've given your heart to the wrong ones and felt discarded.

You've cried silent tears, wondering, "Does anyone even notice I'm hurting?"

But there is One who sees you. One who has never taken His eyes off you. One who has had you on His mind—before you were even formed.

More Than a Thought—A Treasure

Psalm 139:17–18 says:

"How precious also are Your thoughts to me, O God! How vast is the sum of them! Were I to count them, they would outnumber the grains of sand."

Let that sink in.

God's thoughts about you aren't random or fleeting.

AS THE DEER PANTS AFTER THE WATER

They are precious. Constant. Endless.

You were never an afterthought in His heart—you are the desire of it.

You weren't forgotten when you were broken.

You weren't lost when you wandered.

You weren't discarded when others walked away.

You were always on His mind.

God's Love: Personal and Intentional

This love isn't generic. It's specific. Tailored. Deeply personal.

He knows the way you laugh. The way your heart longs for wholeness. The scars you hide. The prayers you whispered and then forgot.

He sees the ache you feel when no one checks in, the longing for someone to care that deeply.

And He does.

He cares about your healing, your hope, your heart.

He's not a distant God with a clipboard—He's an intimate Father with your name engraved on His palm (Isaiah 49:16).

When You Feel Forgotten

When life grows silent, it's easy to believe the lie that God has forgotten you.

But silence isn't absence.

Sometimes the greatest truths are spoken in the quiet:

- "I see you."
- "I've been here all along."
- "You're still Mine."

The same God who crafted the galaxies thinks of you.

The same God who keeps the oceans in place knows your name, your tears, and your timeline.

You're not lost in the crowd.

You are chosen. Loved. Pursued. Remembered.

From the Father's Heart

"Before you were ever broken, I loved you.

Before they ever left, I chose you.

Before your heart ever longed for love, I had already written your name on My heart.

I think about you constantly.

You are not too much. Not too far. Not too forgotten.

You are mine. Always have been. Always will be."

Reflection:

- Have you ever felt forgotten by God?
- What voices have made you feel unseen, and how do they compare to God's voice?
- How does knowing God thinks about you constantly change the way you see yourself?

Journal Prompt:

- When have you felt unseen or forgotten in your life, and how did that experience shape the way you see yourself or God?
- What lies about your worth or significance have you believed because of silence, rejection, or abandonment—and how do those lies compare to what God says about you in Psalm 139:17–18 and Isaiah 49:16?
- If you truly believed that God thinks about you constantly and treasures you deeply, how would it change the way you love yourself, make decisions, and approach relationships?

Prayer:

Father,

Thank You for thinking of me—even when I thought You were far away.

Thank You for being mindful of me in seasons where I felt invisible.

Help me to believe what Your Word says:

That I am seen, I am known, and I am deeply loved.

Teach me to rest in the truth that I was always on Your mind.

Let that truth heal every abandoned place in me.

Amen.

Closing Quote:

"You were never forgotten—you were being remembered in silence."

Chapter Ten: The Prodigal Daughter

Coming back to the arms of the Father—no shame, no guilt, only grace

There comes a moment in every journey when you stop running.

You've tried the world's comforts.

You've poured yourself into the arms of lovers who didn't love you back.

You've silenced the ache with distractions.

You've convinced yourself you were too far gone to go back.

But then, somewhere in the middle of the mess, you hear it:

A whisper. A nudge. A call.

"Daughter, come home."

You Were Never Too Far

Like the prodigal son in Luke 15, maybe you left thinking you'd find something better. Or maybe, like many daughters, you ran because life wounded you in ways that made you question God's love.

You thought He wouldn't want you.

You thought your sin was too big.

You thought your shame disqualified you.

But the Father has been watching the road since the day you left.

He never stopped waiting.

Never stopped hoping.

Never stopped loving.

The moment you even think about coming back, He comes running toward you with open arms.

No lecture. No condemnation. Just grace.

The Enemy Will Say "Stay Away"

Shame has a way of silencing us.

It says, "You should know better."

"You blew your chance."

"You don't deserve another one."

But that's not how your Father speaks.

He says, "I still want you."

"I still choose you."

"I still have a place for you at My table."

There's no shame in coming home—only healing.

There's no guilt in returning—only restoration.

You don't have to clean yourself up first.

You don't have to rehearse your apology.

You just have to come.

Grace Is Greater Than Your Guilt

Maybe you've done things you've never told anyone about.

Maybe the relationship left you broken and bitter.

Maybe you've made vows to never love again.

Maybe you feel numb, dirty, or unworthy.

But the Father's love is not scared of your story.

It runs deeper than your pain.

It reaches further than your sin.

It restores what you thought was too ruined to repair.

This is the power of grace: it doesn't wait for perfection—it meets you in your imperfection and still chooses you.

There's Still a Seat for You

The Father hasn't given your place away.

He hasn't filled your seat at the table.

The robe is still waiting. The ring is still in His hand. The celebration is still being prepared.

You don't need to earn your way back—you just need to say, "Father, I'm ready."

Come back with your heartbreak.

Come back with your regrets.

Come back with your disappointment.

Just come.

From the Father's Heart

"My daughter, I saw every detour and still kept your destiny intact.

I watched you drift but never gave up on you.

You've cried enough. You've wandered long enough.

Come home—not to punishment, but to peace.

I have never stopped loving you.

There is no shame here. Only grace. Come back to Me."

Reflection:

- What has made you feel like God wouldn't want you back?
- Have you been trying to "fix" yourself before returning to Him?
- What would it feel like to run into the arms of God without fear?

Journal Prompt:

- Imagine the Father standing at the gate, arms wide open, waiting just for you. Write a letter to Him—honest, unfiltered, and real.
- Then write what you imagine He would say back to you. Let grace flood the page.

Prayer:

Father,
   I've run for a long time.
   I've tried to hide my brokenness, my mistakes, and my shame.
   But I'm tired. And I miss You.
   Thank You for loving me even when I didn't love myself.
   Thank You for never giving my place away.
   I'm ready to come home—no more hiding, no more guilt.
   Cover me in Your grace and help me walk in freedom again.
   Amen.

Closing Quote:

"Grace didn't wait for you to get it all right. It waited with open arms for you to come home."

Chapter Eleven: Falling in Love with God

What it really means to love the Lord with all your heart, soul, and mind

Y ou've tried everything else—
Poured your love into people who didn't handle it well.
Chased dreams that left you empty.
Clung to relationships that cost you your peace.
But have you ever fully poured your love into God?
We sing that we love Him.
We say we trust Him.
But what does it really mean to fall in love with the One who created our hearts?
This chapter is not about religion.
It's not about performance.
It's about the most sacred, life-altering relationship you'll ever have—
the one where you give God all of you… and finally feel whole.

He's the One You've Been Searching For

You weren't created just to be in love—you were created to be in divine love.

God is not just looking for your obedience—He's longing for your heart.

"You shall love the Lord your God with all your heart and with all your soul and with all your mind." (Matthew 22:37)

He wants you to:

- Talk to Him first thing in the morning.
- Bring your broken pieces to Him—not hide them.
- Trust Him with your future, your desires, your identity.
- Let Him satisfy the craving for love that no man, title, or possession ever could.

Falling in love with God means letting go of partial surrender and giving Him everything—your joy, your wounds, your fears, and your dreams.

Trust is the Doorway to Love

You can't love God deeply until you learn to trust Him.
Many of us love God with hesitation—because people let us down.
We project our past hurts onto Him.
But God is not like them.

- He doesn't abandon.
- He doesn't betray.
- He doesn't lie.

When you begin to trust God with your whole heart, you'll find the freedom to fall in love with Him fully.
You'll stop running to things that break you.
You'll stop hiding the parts of you you're ashamed of.
You'll begin to taste the abundant life He's promised—one filled with joy, peace, and security that no one else can offer.

The More You Know Him, The More You'll Love Him

Falling in love with God isn't a one-time moment—it's a daily pursuit.
  The more you read His Word, the more you'll see His character.
  The more you pray, the more you'll feel His presence.
  The more you listen, the more you'll recognize His voice.
  And soon you'll find:

- He's the safest place for your emotions.
- He's the best friend you've ever had.
- He's the one love who will never let you down.

This Is the Love You Were Made For

You don't have to keep searching.
  The One your soul has longed for… has been longing for you too.
  God doesn't just want a part of your life—He wants to be the center of it.
  He wants you to fall in love with Him the way He's always been in love with you.

Reflection:

- Are there parts of your heart you've held back from God out of fear or mistrust?
- What does "falling in love with God" look like for you in this season?
- What would your life look like if your love for Him became your foundation?

Journal Prompt:

- Write a love letter to God—not as a distant deity, but as the One who knows you deeply and loves you completely. Be honest. Be vulnerable. Let this moment be the beginning (or the deepening) of your love story with Him.

Prayer:

Lord,

I've searched for love in so many places, but I see now that You've been here all along.

I want to know You—not just as God, but as the love of my life.

Teach me to trust You, to lean on You, and to love You with all my heart, soul, and mind.

I surrender the broken places.

I give You my whole heart.

Help me fall deeply, madly, unshakably in love with You.

Amen.

Closing Quote:

"The greatest romance you'll ever experience is falling in love with the One who loved you first—and never stopped."

Chapter Twelve: A Love That Transforms

Becoming whole, healed, and ready to love again—on God's terms

You've cried.

You've released.

You've let go of toxic love and walked through the wilderness of loneliness.

You've sat with the pain.

You've wrestled with your desires.

You've discovered how deeply God loves you.

And now—you're no longer the same.

This is the love that transforms.

But here's the shift:

You're not being healed just so you can love someone again—

You're being healed so you can love God's way… with wholeness, wisdom, and discernment.

Too many times we've loved on our own terms:

- From our brokenness.
- From our need to be validated.
- From our fear of being alone.
- From our desire to feel wanted—even if it meant settling.

But when you've been transformed by God's love, your standards change.

Your vision clears.

Your heart gets stronger.

And you no longer crave love that costs you your identity, peace, or purpose.

Love on God's Terms Looks Like This:

- Peace, not pressure.
- Patience, not performance.
- Truth, not manipulation.
- Purpose, not confusion.
- Partnership, not possession.

God's love doesn't just heal you.

It teaches you how to recognize real love—because now you know what it feels like to be seen, known, and deeply valued.

You won't be fooled by counterfeit connections anymore.

You won't entertain people who only want pieces of you.

You won't stay where you have to shrink.

Because God didn't just bandage your wounds—

He restored your vision.

He renewed your heart.

He made you whole.

Your Wholeness Is a Weapon

The enemy wanted you to keep repeating cycles.

To stay trapped in the familiar.

To doubt your worth.

But God used the wilderness to transform you from the inside out.

Now you're not walking into love from a place of desperation—

You're walking in healed, whole, and submitted to God's timing.

You're no longer asking, "Who will love me?"

You're now asking, "Who is worthy of the healed me?"

You're Ready—but on God's Terms

You may feel ready to love again.

But you're not in a rush—because you've learned that love without God's hand on it is dangerous.

You've learned that God's "no" is protection.

His "wait" is preparation.

And His "yes" comes with peace, alignment, and confirmation.

God isn't withholding love from you.

He's preparing a love for you—and preparing you for it.

Reflection:

- Have you been trying to define love based on your own terms—or God's?
- What does a God-centered, healthy love look like to you now?
- How has your view of love changed since the beginning of this journey?

Journal Prompt:

- Write down the qualities of a relationship that align with God's standards.
- Then write a prayer surrendering your desire for love to Him, trusting that He knows what you need better than you do.

Prayer:

Father,

Thank You for not just healing me—but for transforming me.

I surrender my ideas of love, my timeline, and my desires to You.

Help me to love the way You love—fully, purely, and patiently.

Teach me how to wait well, to guard my heart, and to walk in wholeness.

I trust that when the time is right, the love You've prepared for me will reflect the love You've already poured into me.

Amen.

Closing Quote:

"You are no longer searching for love—because now you are walking in the love that changes everything."

Chapter Thirteen: You Are Worth the Wait

Embracing singleness as sacred preparation, not punishment

It's quiet sometimes.

And not just in your home, but in your heart.

You scroll your phone and see couples. Engagements. Families.

And a small voice inside whispers, "When will it be my turn?"

Singleness can feel like a sentence when your heart desires connection.

It can feel like God has forgotten you.

But what if this season isn't a punishment...

What if it's a divine pause—full of purpose?

Singleness is Not a Holding Cell—It's a Holy Process

This time alone is not meant to break you, but to build you.

Not to deprive you, but to prepare you.

You are not waiting for someone to complete you—you are learning how to walk in fullness so you don't settle for someone who drains you.

Yes, the process is hard.

Yes, there are nights when loneliness feels unbearable.

Yes, there are moments you question if God even hears you.

But let's be honest—

You've been in relationships where you felt more alone than you do now.

You've shared your body and still felt empty.

You've lowered your standards, hoping to feel wanted, and ended up wounded.

So, now you choose differently.

Not because it's easy.

But because you finally believe the truth:

You are worth the wait.

Don't Settle Just to Escape the Silence

Settling may silence your loneliness for a moment,
   but it can suffocate your purpose for years.
   God doesn't just want you in love—
   He wants you in the right love.
   A love that points you to Him.
   A love that reflects His heart, not just your desires.
   So if waiting feels painful,
   remember this: waiting with God is always safer than rushing without Him.

Surrendering What You Can't See

This is where trust gets real.
   You may not see the full picture.
   You may not have all the answers.
   But God is asking for your surrender—not your strategy.
   Because while you're worried about "when" it will happen,
   God is focused on who you are becoming.
   You're becoming wiser.
   Stronger.
   More rooted in your identity.
   And better prepared to love without losing yourself.

It's Not About Being Alone—It's About Being Available

God is not making you wait to torment you.

He's using this season to align your life with Heaven.

To teach you how to love Him with your whole heart

so that when He sends someone, you don't make them your god.

You are not forgotten.

You are being refined, not rejected.

Held, not hidden.

And God—your Father, your Creator, your Lover—hasn't taken His eyes off you.

Reflection:

- Have you viewed singleness as a punishment instead of preparation?
- What fears or insecurities do you need to surrender to God in this season?
- How is God inviting you to trust Him even when the future feels uncertain?

Journal Prompt:

- Write a letter to yourself declaring the value of this season.
- Affirm your worth. Acknowledge the hard moments.
- And speak over your life the truth that God has not forgotten you—He's preparing something beautiful.

Prayer:

God,

This season of waiting can feel heavy.

But I choose to trust You with what I cannot see.

Help me surrender my timeline, my desires, and my fears.

Teach me to embrace singleness as sacred, not shameful.

Remind me that I am not behind—I am exactly where You need me to be.

Give me strength to wait well, and peace to know that Your plans for me are worth every minute I've spent alone.

Amen.

Closing Quote:

"You are not waiting for love—you are being prepared for the love that won't require you to shrink, settle, or stray from God."

Chapter Fourteen: Becoming His Bride

Living daily in intimacy with the One who calls you Beloved

You've searched for love in many faces. You've bent yourself to fit into the arms of people who never truly held you.

You've given away parts of yourself, hoping someone would finally see your worth.

But through all the pain, all the heartbreak, and all the emptiness…

Jesus never stopped loving you.

While you were chasing approval,

He was preparing a place for you at His feet.

While you were crying yourself to sleep,

He was singing songs of deliverance over you.

While you were falling apart,

He was waiting to make you whole.

He Calls You "Mine"

You are not forgotten.

You are not too far gone.

You are not too broken to be chosen.

Your past didn't scare Him.

Your wounds didn't repel Him.
Your mess didn't cancel your worth.
He still calls you Beloved.
He still says, "You are Mine."
And now, He invites you into the most sacred relationship of your life—
To become His Bride.
Not just in word, but in heart.
Not just in public worship, but in private surrender.
Not just when you feel good, but when you feel empty.

An Invitation to Intimacy

This is not a fairytale—it's a divine reality.
   Jesus desires you.
   Not just to be near Him, but to walk with Him daily—
   to talk, cry, laugh, grow, rest, and worship in His presence.
   This is not about religion.
   It's about relationship.
   A love affair with the One who wrote your story before you took your first breath.
   You are not chasing after love anymore.
   Love is chasing after you.

Prophetic Encouragement: You Will Make It

Daughter, you will make it.
   You will heal.
   You will rise.
   You will dance again.
   You will trust again.
   You will love again.
   Not from desperation,
   but from a place of divine wholeness.

You will no longer shrink to be chosen.

You will no longer bleed for love that isn't real.

You will no longer search for something you already have in Christ.

Because you are already loved.

Already seen.

Already chosen.

Stop Searching—Start Receiving

Stop trying to convince people to love you when the King of Heaven already does.

Stop striving to be "enough" when God made you more than enough in Him.

Stop chasing the temporary when the eternal is waiting for you to come home.

Beloved, He's waiting for your heart.

And He has more to offer you than this world ever could.

Let today be the day you stop reaching for man's love

and rest in the arms of the One who loved you first—and loves you most.

Reflection:

- What have you been running to for love and acceptance?
- How can you begin to shift your heart toward intimacy with God daily?
- In what areas do you still struggle to believe that you are already loved?

Journal Prompt:

- Write a love letter back to God.
- Thank Him for loving you in your worst.
- Tell Him where it still hurts—and allow Him to speak healing into those places.
- Begin a new rhythm of responding to His love instead of performing for

it.

Prayer:

Father,

Thank You for loving me like no one else ever has.

Thank You for pursuing me even when I walked away.

Heal the places in me that believed I had to earn love.

Teach me how to live as Your bride—daily, intimately, passionately.

Help me to stop chasing what doesn't satisfy, and fully embrace the love that never runs out.

I give You all of me… again.

In Jesus' name,

Amen.

Closing Quote:

"You don't have to chase what God has already given—love Himself has chosen you."

Healing Exercise: A Bridal Encounter with God

Purpose:

To help you feel chosen, see yourself as beloved, and step into divine intimacy by releasing false identities and embracing your place as the Bride of Christ.

Step 1: Set the Atmosphere

- Find a quiet, undisturbed space.
- Light a candle or play soft instrumental worship music.
- Have a journal, pen, and Bible nearby.
- Close your eyes and take a few deep breaths. Whisper, "I am His Beloved."

Step 2: Release False Names

In your journal, make a list of all the names or labels the world, relationships, or trauma have placed on you.

Write them down honestly—names like: Unworthy. Forgotten. Used. Unlovable. Rejected. Not Enough.

Now, draw a bold line through each one.

Speak out loud:

"This is not who I am. I am not what they did. I am not what they said. I am who God says I am."

Step 3: Receive Your Bridal Identity

Now, write a new list. This time, write who you are in Christ:

- Chosen
- Loved
- Forgiven
- Covered
- Radiant
- Worth the wait
- His Bride

After each word, say:

"I receive this truth about myself."

Imagine Jesus placing a pure white robe on you and whispering,

"You are Mine. Beautiful, radiant, and redeemed."

Step 4: Prophetic Visualization – The Bridal Walk

Close your eyes again. Picture yourself walking down an aisle, but not toward a man. You're walking toward Jesus—glorious, smiling, arms open wide.

He's not disappointed.

He's not angry.

He's not ashamed of you.

He's delighted. He's been waiting for you.

As you reach Him, He takes your hand and whispers:

"You are altogether beautiful, My darling. There is no flaw in you." (Song of Songs 4:7)

Sit with that image. Breathe it in. Write down how it made you feel.

Step 5: Daily Intimacy Commitment

Write a personal vow to the Lord, like a bride would to her Groom.

Example:

"Today, I vow to walk closely with You. I will seek You daily. I will not hide when I'm broken, but bring my heart to You. I choose You—not just in moments of desperation, but in every part of life. You are my One True Love."

Hang it somewhere you'll see it often.

Affirmation to Speak Aloud:

"I am not waiting to be loved—I already am.

I am not chasing worth—I was born with it.

I belong to the One who made me, sees me, knows me...

And still calls me His Bride."

Chapter 15: Drink Deeply

"O taste and see that the Lord is good: blessed is the woman who trusts in Him." – Psalm 34:8

There comes a time in every woman's life when she must decide: Will I keep chasing empty wells, or will I finally drink from the One who promises living water? If you've come this far, then I believe you're standing at that very moment.

This is your invitation.

Not from me—but from the God who saw you crying in the midnight hour, the One who watched over you when you were left, betrayed, and broken. He is not asking you to perform. He's not requiring perfection. All He wants is for you to trust Him... deeply. Fully. Even just a mustard seed of faith is enough for Him to work with.

I dare you to trust Him.

I dare you to take Him at His word. He said, "I have never seen the righteous forsaken, nor His seed begging for bread." And I am living proof that He keeps His promises.

Testimonies of Trust

Tasha's Story:

"I spent years thinking I had to settle—settle for being someone's second choice, settle for love that came with bruises, lies, and silence. But one day, I fell on my knees and whispered a simple prayer: 'God, help me.' That day changed my life. I didn't see instant results, but peace began to flood my heart like I had never known. Today, I'm walking in freedom. No longer begging for love—I'm overflowing with it."

Keisha's Story:

"My heart was shattered after a five-year relationship ended with betrayal. I felt humiliated and hopeless. But instead of rebounding into another dead-end situation, I waited. I pressed into God. I journaled, I worshiped, I cried—and He met me there. Two years later, not only is my heart healed, but I'm leading a women's ministry, helping others find the same freedom. God turned my mourning into dancing."

Danielle's Story:

"I used to believe I was too far gone, that after all the mistakes I'd made, God wouldn't want anything to do with me. But the moment I decided to take Him seriously—really trust Him—He began to rebuild me. Piece by piece, day by day. Now I wake up with purpose. I smile without faking it. He gave me beauty for ashes."

God Will Satisfy Every Need

I've been where you are—broken, afraid, unsure if I could ever truly be whole. But I want you to know: God has always met my needs. Always. Even when I didn't understand the process, He was working behind the scenes. He's been my provider, my healer, my comforter, my friend. And He wants to be all that and more to you.

Let this truth settle in your soul:

The pain you've experienced is not punishment—it's preparation.

God is preparing you for greatness, for joy, for impact. He's stretching your capacity so you can carry more of His purpose. Nothing you've been through will be wasted.

Drink Deeply. Live Fully.

This isn't just the end of a book. It's the beginning of a beautiful new chapter in your life. A life rooted in the love of God. A life that no longer runs on empty. You've been thirsty for so long. You've tried everything else. Now it's time to drink deeply from the well that never runs dry.

You can do this.

Healing is yours.

Wholeness is yours.

Love—real, pure, unconditional—is yours.

All you have to do is say yes.

Reflection

- Where have you been running to for fulfillment?
- What would it look like to fully trust God with your heart, your pain, and your future?
- Journal Prompt
- Write a letter to God as if He is the only One who can satisfy your soul. Be honest. Be bold. Be vulnerable. Then listen for His response.

Closing Prayer

Father,

I'm tired of running to broken wells. I want You. I want Your living water. Quench every part of me that has been parched by pain, disappointment, and fear. Teach me to trust You—not just with the easy parts of my life, but with the deep, wounded places too. I say yes to You, Lord. I believe that my best is ahead of me. Amen.

Final Quote:

"You may have been broken, but now you are being rebuilt by the hands of the One who makes all things new."

Chapter Fifteen: Drink Deeply

The Invitation to Experience God's Love Like Living Water—Satisfying Every Need

"O taste and see that the Lord is good; blessed is the woman who trusts in Him." — Psalm 34:8

There comes a moment in every woman's healing journey when she has to make a sacred decision:

Will I keep running to broken wells... or will I finally drink from the One who never runs dry?

Because if we're honest, we've all had seasons where we were thirsty— not just physically, but emotionally... spiritually... soul-deep thirsty.

Thirsty to be chosen.

Thirsty to be wanted.

Thirsty to feel safe.

Thirsty to be held without being handled.

Thirsty to be loved without fear, confusion, compromise, or pain.

And when you've been thirsty for a long time, **anything that looks like water will tempt you.**

Even if it's poison.

Even if it's temporary.

Even if it leaves you emptier than before.

That's what counterfeit love does.

It promises satisfaction, but it produces cravings.

It gives you attention, but steals your peace.

It holds you for a moment, then abandons you with a deeper ache.

But God is calling you higher now.

This chapter is your invitation to stop sipping from what drains you... and start drinking deeply from what restores you.

Broken Wells Can't Hold Living Water

Some of us have tried to drink from:

- People who were never emotionally available
- Relationships that required you to shrink to be kept
- Validation that disappears when your beauty fades or your mood changes
- Attention that felt good, but didn't feel safe
- Temporary comfort that cost you long-term wholeness

And every time you drank from those places, you walked away thirsty again.

Scripture says in **Jeremiah 2:13**, God's people committed two evils:

They **forsook Him, the fountain of living waters**, and carved out broken cisterns that can't hold water.

That's what happens when we turn to things that can't sustain us.

You were never created to survive off crumbs.

You were created to overflow.

Jesus Doesn't Offer You a Distraction—He Offers You Living Water

In **John 4**, Jesus meets a woman at a well.

And without condemning her, He exposes her thirst.

She had been married five times and was living with a man who wasn't her husband.

But Jesus didn't approach her with shame.

He approached her with an invitation:

"Whoever drinks of the water that I shall give him will never thirst." (John 4:14)

That doesn't mean you'll never desire love again.

It means you'll stop craving it from places that break you.

It means your soul will finally find a Source.

Because **God doesn't just want to heal the wounds of your past—He wants to satisfy the thirst underneath them.**

What Happens When You Drink Deeply

When you drink deeply from God's love, something shifts.

- You stop chasing what doesn't choose you.
- You stop begging for love that requires you to prove your worth.
- You stop confusing intensity with intimacy.
- Peace becomes more attractive than chaos.
- You stop settling for attention when you desire covenant.
- Because you finally know your value.
- You stop numbing your pain and start surrendering it.
- You learn the difference between coping and healing.
- You stop making people your source.
- You stop expecting humans to fill what only God was designed to fill.

And that's where freedom lives—

not in being perfect, but in being **full**.

This Isn't the End of the Book—It's the Beginning of Your Overflow

If you've made it here, it means you've survived:

- heartbreak
- disappointment
- loneliness
- spiritual warfare
- temptation
- cycles
- counterfeits
- and seasons where you didn't even recognize yourself

But you kept going.
And now God is saying:
"Daughter, stop sipping. Drink deeply."
Not just in church.
Not just when you're desperate.
But daily—consistently—intimately.
Drink from His presence.
Drink from His Word.
Drink from prayer.
Drink from worship.
Drink from stillness.
Drink until your soul remembers what it feels like to be whole.

Testimonies of Trust

Tasha's Story

"I spent years thinking I had to settle—settle for being someone's second choice, settle for love that came with bruises, lies, and silence. But one day, I fell on my knees and whispered a simple prayer: 'God, help me.' That day changed my life. I didn't see instant results, but peace began to flood my heart like I had never known. Today, I'm walking in freedom. No longer begging for love—I'm overflowing with it."

Keisha's Story

"My heart was shattered after a five-year relationship ended with betrayal. I felt humiliated and hopeless. But instead of rebounding into another dead-end situation, I waited. I pressed into God. I journaled, I worshiped, I cried—and He met me there. Two years later, not only is my heart healed, but I'm leading a women's ministry, helping others find the same freedom. God turned my mourning into dancing."

Danielle's Story

"I used to believe I was too far gone, that after all the mistakes I'd made, God wouldn't want anything to do with me. But the moment I decided to take Him seriously—really trust Him—He began to rebuild me. Piece by piece, day by day. Now I wake up with purpose. I smile without faking it. He gave me beauty for ashes."

God Will Satisfy Every Need

Let this truth settle in your spirit:

God is not just a part of your healing—He is the Source of it.

He is your:

- Provider

- Comforter
- Protector
- Restorer
- Healer
- Redeemer
- Friend
- Lover of your soul

And He doesn't just want to meet some needs.

He wants to heal the place that *keeps needing the wrong things.*

The pain you experienced was not punishment—it was preparation.

God is stretching your capacity so you can carry more of His presence, more of His purpose, and more of His peace.

Nothing you've been through will be wasted.

A Word from the Father's Heart

"My daughter, I have watched you drink from wells that could not satisfy you.

I saw every time you reached for love and came back empty.

But I never condemned you—I waited for you.

I am the fountain you've been searching for.

I don't just want to heal you—I want to fill you.

I want to satisfy the thirst underneath your tears.

Come closer. Drink deeply.

Let Me love you until you no longer crave what breaks you."

Reflection

- Where have you been running for fulfillment instead of running to God?
- What "broken wells" have you tried to drink from, hoping they would satisfy you?
- What would it look like to trust God with your heart, your pain, and your future—fully?

Journal Prompt

Write a letter to God as if He is the only One who can satisfy your soul.
Be honest. Be bold. Be vulnerable.
Then write what you sense God responding back to you—
not from fear, but from His love.

Closing Prayer

Father,
I'm tired of running to broken wells.
I'm tired of reaching for what looks like water but leaves me thirsty again.
Today, I choose You—fully.
Quench every part of me that has been parched by pain, disappointment,
fear, and rejection.
Teach me to trust You—not just with the easy parts of my life,
but with the deep, wounded places too.
I say yes to Your love.
I say yes to Your healing.
I say yes to Your timing.
And I believe that my best is ahead of me.
Fill me until I overflow.
In Jesus' name, Amen.

Closing Quote

"You may have been broken, but now you are being rebuilt by the hands of
the One who makes all things new."

Final Letter from God

My Beloved Daughter,

I've seen every moment—every heartbreak, every question, every time you felt like giving up. But I never left your side. I've walked with you through every valley and stood guard over you when you didn't even know you were in danger.

I've been patiently waiting for you to stop chasing love that can't satisfy, and turn back to Me—the One who loves you without condition or expiration.

You don't have to earn My love.

You don't have to fix yourself to be worthy of My embrace.

You are already Mine—just as you are.

I want to pour out living water on your dry places.

I want to heal the wounds you've hidden.

I want to fill you with peace that no storm can steal.

All I ask is this: trust Me.

Let Me love you.

Let Me lead you.

Let Me restore all that has been lost.

The life I've planned for you is far greater than anything you've left behind.

So come closer.

Drink deeply.

Rest in My love.

You are chosen. You are cherished. You are never forgotten.

Love always,

Your Heavenly Father

Final Word from the Author

Dear Sister,

If you've made it to this point, I want to look you in the eyes—heart to heart—and say: I'm proud of you. Not because you've had it all together, but because you've chosen to keep going when quitting felt easier. Because you dared to open your heart, peel back the pain, and let God in.

I wrote this book from the depths of my own healing journey. Not from a place of perfection, but from the cracks where God's light poured in. I want you to know: you are not alone, and your pain has not been wasted. Every tear you've cried has been seen. Every silent prayer, heard. And every piece of your brokenness is being gathered by a God who still has a plan for your life.

Keep showing up. Keep trusting. Keep drinking deeply from the well of His love.

And when doubt whispers, when loneliness creeps in, or when you're tempted to go back to what once broke you—remember this: You are worth the wait. God's best is worth the wait. And your healing is already in motion.

I believe in you.

Now go and live like you believe in you, too.

With all my love and prayers,
Chanita R. Ramsey
Your sister in healing and wholeness